RIVER CAFE
POCKET BOOKS
FISH &
SHELLFISH

RIVER CAFE
POCKET BOOKS
FISH &
SHELLFISH

ROSE GRAY AND RUTH ROGERS

Introduction

Every region of Italy has its own way of cooking fish and the recipes in this book reflect these regional differences. For simplicity, we have divided the chapters by the methods of cooking – grilling, roasting, frying and poaching – appropriate to each fish.

In Liguria, where the fish is mostly small, fresh anchovies and sardines are fried in different ways. On the Tuscan coast and down to Rome, fish such as sea bass and red mullet are nearly always grilled whole. And raw fish has become increasingly popular – in Puglia we ate raw tuna cut thickly with bruschetta, and in the Veneto lovely sweet langoustine carpaccio served with a ripe, fruity olive oil. Every region has its own way of preparing salt cod. Travelling throughout Italy we have learned that the way you serve fish depends on where you are.

A good fishmonger will have a wide variety of fish and be willing to prepare it in the way you require for your recipe. Most importantly the fish must be fresh. Look for bright eyes, scarlet gills, firm flesh and shiny scales. The stiffer the fish, the better. You may enjoy preparing and filleting the fish yourself – with this in mind we have given instructions on how to do so at the end of the book.

All recipes serve four unless otherwise stated. All herbs are fresh unless otherwise stated. All eggs are large, free-range, organic unless otherwise stated. Wash all fresh herbs, fruits and vegetables in cold water before use.

CHAPTER ONE
RAW FISH

| Sea bass carpaccio

2.5kg Sea bass, filleted • 8 Cherry tomatoes, halved • Juice of 2 lemons, plus 1 lemon cut into quarters • 3 Dried red chillies, crumbled • 3 tbs Marjoram leaves • Extra virgin olive oil

Place the bass fillets skin-side down on a board. Using a long-bladed knife, cut into slices as finely as you can along the whole length of the fillet. Place the slices side by side on cold plates.

Squeeze the juice and some pulp out of the tomatoes over the bass. The tomato acids will 'cook' the fish. Drizzle with the lemon juice, season and add a few flakes of chilli. Drizzle with olive oil and scatter over the marjoram leaves. Serve with the lemon quarters.

2 | Raw tuna bruschetta

500g Tuna loin, trimmed of skin and sinew • 2 Dried red chillies, crumbled • 1 Lemon, cut into quarters • Extra virgin olive oil

Bruschetta
4 Slices of sourdough bread • 1 Garlic clove, peeled • Extra virgin olive oil

Cut the tuna across the grain into slices 5mm thick.

For the bruschetta, grill the bread on both sides. Rub one side lightly with the garlic clove, season and drizzle with olive oil.

Serve the tuna raw beside the bruschetta,
sprinkled with the chillies, black pepper and sea salt.
Serve with the lemon quarters.

3 Langoustine carpaccio

*16 Live langoustines • Juice of 1 lemon, plus 2 lemons,
cut in half*

Put the langoustines on a board and, with a sharp
knife, cut lengthways from the head down. You want
to 'butterfly' them, not cut all the way through. Season.
Squeeze over the lemon juice and serve immediately
with the lemon halves.

Langoustine carpaccio (Recipe 3)

4 Fresh anchovies with chilli

500g Fresh anchovies, filleted • 1 Dried red chilli, crumbled • 2 tbs Finely chopped flat-leaf parsley • Juice of 4 lemons• Extra virgin olive oil

In a serving dish, arrange a layer of anchovies side by side, not overlapping, and sprinkle with a little sea salt, black pepper, chilli and parsley. Pour over a generous amount of lemon juice – this is what 'cooks' the anchovies – and some olive oil. Repeat the layers, ensuring the top layer is covered with oil and lemon.

Cover with cling film and leave to marinate for at least 1 hour before serving with bruschetta (see Recipe 2).

5 Fresh anchovies with rosemary

*500g Fresh anchovies, filleted • 1 Rosemary sprig •
1 tsp Fennel seeds, ground • 1 Dried red chilli,
crumbled • Juice of 2 lemons • 3 tbs Red wine vinegar
• Extra virgin olive oil*

Finely chop the rosemary and mix it with 1 tbs of sea
salt. In a serving dish, arrange a layer of anchovies
skin-side up, packing them closely together. Sprinkle
over the rosemary, fennel, chilli and some black
pepper. Pour over the lemon juice – this is what
'cooks' the anchovies – the vinegar and some olive oil.
Cover with cling film and leave to marinate for at least
1 hour before serving with bruschetta (see Recipe 2).

CHAPTER TWO
GRILLED FISH

6 Grilled sea bass brushed with rosemary and olive oil

2kg Whole sea bass, scaled and cleaned • 2 Rosemary branches • 1 Lemon, cut into quarters • Extra virgin olive oil

Preheat a grill, griddle pan or barbecue.

Season the inside of the fish. Put one rosemary branch in the cavity and lightly rub olive oil over the fish, especially on the tail. Generously season the outside of the fish.

Put 6 tbs of olive oil in a small bowl. Place the fish on the preheated grill and brush it with the second rosemary branch dipped in the oil. Turn it over after about 8 minutes, brush again and season. Cook for a further 8 minutes, brushing the fish as it cooks.

Put the fish on a serving plate. Serve with the lemon quarters.

7 Grilled whole baby squid

600g Baby squid, cleaned • 3 tbs Roughly chopped marjoram • 2 Dried red chillies, crumbled • Juice of 1 lemon, plus 1 lemon cut into quarters • Extra virgin olive oil

Preheat a grill, griddle pan or barbecue.

Season the squid generously, inside and out. Push 1 tsp of marjoram inside each sac.

For the sauce, mix the chillies with 1 tsp of the lemon juice, 2 tbs of olive oil and the remaining marjoram. Season.

Place the squid bodies and tentacles on the hot grill and squeeze over a little lemon juice.

When the flesh is lightly charred, turn immediately and grill on the other side. Serve with the sauce and the lemon quarters.

8   Grilled squid, chilli and rocket

4 Medium squid, cleaned • Fresh Red Chilli Sauce (see Recipe 90) • 200g Rocket • Juice of 1 lemon, plus 1 lemon cut into quarters • Extra virgin olive oil

Preheat a grill, griddle pan or barbecue to very hot.

Using a serrated knife, score the inner side of each flattened squid body with parallel lines 1cm apart, and then equally apart the other way to make cross-hatching. Place the squid and tentacles scored-side down on the grill and season. Grill for 1-2 minutes. Turn the pieces over. Turn again and the pieces will immediately curl up, by which time they will be cooked.

Combine 6 tbs of olive oil with the lemon juice in a bowl and season. Toss with the rocket leaves.

Put the squid and tentacles on a plate with the rocket. Spoon the chilli sauce over the squid and serve with the lemon quarters.

9   Grilled halibut

4 Halibut steaks, 2-3cm thick • 2 Lemons, cut into quarters • Salsa Verde (see Recipe 80) • Extra virgin olive oil

Preheat a grill, griddle pan or barbecue to hot.

Lightly season the halibut on both sides and brush with olive oil. Place the fish on the grill and cook for

2 minutes, or until it comes away easily from the grill and is lightly browned. Turn over and grill on the other side for 2 minutes.

Squeeze over a little lemon juice and serve with salsa verde and the lemon quarters.

10 Grilled turbot

4 x 220g Turbot fillets • Salsa Verde (see Recipe 80) • 1 Lemon, cut into quarters • Extra virgin olive oil

Preheat a grill, griddle pan or barbecue.

Brush the flesh side of the fillets with olive oil, season, and put on the grill for 3-4 minutes. Turn over and grill for another 3-4 minutes. Serve with salsa verde and the lemon quarters.

11 Seared salmon

4 x 250g Wild salmon fillets • 1 Lemon, cut into quarters • Extra virgin olive oil

Preheat a grill, griddle pan or barbecue.

Season the fillets of salmon and grill, skin-side down, for about a minute, until just seared. Turn over and sear the flesh side for a minute – the fish will be cooked rare. Drizzle over olive oil and serve with the lemon quarters.

12 Grilled monkfish

4 x 250g Monkfish fillets • Juice of 1 lemon, plus 1 lemon cut into quarters • Salsa Verde (see Recipe 80) • Extra virgin olive oil

Preheat a grill, griddle pan or barbecue.

To butterfly the monkfish, place one hand flat over the top of the fat end of each fillet. Using a sharp knife, cut into the fillet horizontally about three-quarters of the way through so that it butterflies out. Score it lightly with the knife.

Place the butterflied fillets on a plate, squeeze the lemon juice over, season and drizzle over olive oil. Grill for 3-4 minutes on each side.

Serve with the lemon quarters and salsa verde.

13 Grilled sea bass stuffed with herbs and lemon

4 x 220g Sea bass fillets • 2 tbs Each of marjoram, basil or mint, green fennel herb or dill, roughly chopped • Juice of 1 lemon, plus 1 lemon cut into quarters • Extra virgin olive oil

Preheat a grill, griddle pan or barbecue.

Make 1 cm-deep slashes across the width of the skin side of the fillets. Season the fish. Mix the herbs together and push this mixture into the slashes.

Place the fillets on the grill, skin-side down, and grill for 4 minutes. Turn over and grill for a further 4 minutes or until cooked.

Mix the lemon juice with 100ml olive oil, pour it over the grilled fish and scatter any remaining herbs over. Serve with the lemon quarters.

---

14 Seared marinated tuna

4 x 220g Tuna steaks • 3 Garlic cloves, peeled and finely chopped • 2 tbs Chopped green fennel herb • 1 tbs Fennel seeds, ground • 2 Small dried red chillies, crumbled • 200ml White wine • Juice of 1 lemon, plus 1 lemon cut into quarters • Extra virgin olive oil

Place the tuna steaks on a board. Rub half the garlic, fennel, fennel seeds, chillies and some salt and pepper into the fish. Turn it over and do the same on the other side.

Place the steaks side by side in a flat container and pour in the white wine, lemon juice and 100ml olive oil. Cover and leave to marinate in a cool place for at least 1 hour.

Preheat a grill, griddle or barbecue to very hot. Dry the tuna steaks with kitchen towel and sear on the grill for 1 minute on each side.

Serve with the lemon quarters.

Seared marinated tuna (Recipe 14)

15 Monkfish spiedini with pancetta

800g Monkfish, cut into sixteen 3cm cubes •
12 Pancetta slices • 2 tbs Chopped green fennel herb
• 2 Lemons, cut into quarters • Extra virgin olive oil

Put the monkfish in a bowl with the fennel and season. Add 3 tbs of olive oil and stir. Marinate in the fridge for 15 minutes.

Preheat a grill, griddle pan or barbecue.

Fold each pancetta slice into 3, approximately the same size as the monkfish. Using 4 wooden, metal or rosemary-stick skewers, thread on the monkfish, alternating it with the pancetta, 4 pieces of fish and 3 of pancetta per skewer.

Grill the spiedini carefully, about 8 minutes, turning from time to time. Serve with the lemon quarters.

16 Monkfish spiedini with scallops

350g Monkfish tail, boned, skinned and cut into cubes the same size as the scallops • 8 Medium scallops •
4 x 15cm Rosemary branches • Anchovy and Rosemary Sauce (see Recipe 79) • 2 Lemons, cut into quarters

Preheat a grill, griddle pan or barbecue.

Pull the leaves off the rosemary stalks, leaving just the tufts at the end. Sharpen the other end into a point.

Thread a scallop onto a rosemary stalk, making sure the stalk goes through the white muscle part and the coral. Thread on a piece of monkfish, another scallop, and then another piece of monkfish.

Place the spiedini on the grill and season. Turn over after 3 minutes or when the spiedini no longer stick but have sealed and are brown. Grill for a further few minutes.

Serve with the anchovy and rosemary sauce and lemon quarters.

17 Grilled scallops

16 Scallops • 1 Lemon, cut into quarters • Extra virgin olive oil

Preheat a grill, griddle pan or barbecue.

Season the scallops very generously on both sides with salt and pepper. Place on the grill until lightly brown and crisp, then turn over and grill the other side. The scallops should be tender on the inside and crisp on the surface. Serve with the lemon quarters and a drizzle of olive oil, or with Anchovy and Rosemary Sauce (see Recipe 79).

18 Grilled tuna carpaccio

1kg Tuna loin, trimmed of skin and sinew • 2 Fresh red chillies, cut in half lengthways, de-seeded and finely sliced • Juice of 3 lemons, plus 2 lemons cut into quarters • 100g Rocket • Extra virgin olive oil

Preheat a griddle pan to very hot.

Cover a board with a mixture of sea salt and coarsely ground black pepper. Roll the tuna loin in this to cover the surfaces with a thick crust. Place the loin on the hot griddle and seal briefly on all sides. The salt and pepper should cook into the surface, making a coat. The flesh should remain raw. Leave to cool.

Using a large, thick-bladed knife, kept damp with a wet cloth, cut very thin slices from the tuna loin. Wet the knife each time you make a slice. Arrange the tuna on 4 plates in one layer. Sprinkle over the chillies, squeeze over plenty of lemon juice and season generously. Place a few rocket leaves over the tuna, drizzle with olive oil and serve with the lemon quarters.

19 Grilled langoustine

16 Langoustines • 2 Lemons, cut into quarters

Fennel and chilli sauce
4 Green herb tops of fennel bulbs, or a handful of fresh fennel herb, finely chopped • 1 Fennel bulb, tough outer layer removed, finely chopped • 3 Fresh red chillies, cut

in half lengthways, de-seeded and finely chopped •
Juice of 1 lemon • Extra virgin olive oil

Preheat a grill, griddle pan or barbecue to very hot.

For the sauce, put the green fennel tops, fennel bulb and chillies in a bowl. Add the lemon juice and leave for 5 minutes. Add 5 tbs of olive oil and season with salt and pepper.

Grill the langoustines for 2-3 minutes on each side. Serve with the lemon quarters and the sauce.

20 Grilled whole side of salmon

Serves 8

1 x 4kg Wild salmon, trimmed and filleted • 2 Lemons,
cut into quarters • Extra virgin olive oil

Preheat a grill, griddle pan or barbecue.

Season both sides of the salmon and rub with olive oil.

Place the salmon skin-side down on the grill and cook for 4 minutes. Turn over and grill for a further 3 minutes. The fish should be rare in the middle.

Place on a platter, skin-side up. Drizzle with olive oil and cut into thick slices. Serve with the lemon quarters.

Grilled whole side of salmon (Recipe 20)

21 Grilled red mullet crostini

4 x 500g Red mullet • 4 Salted anchovies, rinsed and finely chopped • Juice of 1 lemon, plus 3 cut into quarters • 1 tbs Finely chopped rosemary leaves • 100g Small black olives, stoned and finely chopped • 1 Dried red chilli, crumbled • 2 tbs Thyme leaves • 1 Ciabatta loaf, sliced • 2 Garlic cloves, peeled • Extra virgin olive oil

Preheat a grill, griddle pan or barbecue.

Put the anchovies into a bowl and mix with the lemon juice. Add the rosemary and season with pepper. Add 2 tbs of olive oil and mix well.

Put the olives, chilli and thyme in a separate bowl and add enough olive oil to make a rough paste.

Season the mullet on all sides, brush with olive oil and grill, about 5 minutes on each side.

Grill the ciabatta on both sides, rub with garlic and drizzle with olive oil.

Put each mullet on a plate with the crostini, and spread half with anchovy and half with olives. Serve with the lemon quarters.

Red mullet is one of the strongest flavoured fish. The anchovies and olives in this recipe make this a spicy combination. If you can find the baby mullet – which are more delicate – use 2-3 per portion. It is always important to keep these beautiful bright pink fish whole, regardless of size.

22 Grilled flattened sardines

16 Sardines, trimmed, filleted and flattened •
4 Dried red chillies, crumbled • Grated zest of 3
lemons, plus 2 cut into quarters • Extra virgin olive oil

Preheat the barbecue, griddle pan or grill.

Rub the flesh of the sardines with chilli, salt,
pepper and lemon zest. Place skin-side down on
the preheated grill, and cook for 1-2 minutes.
Turn over and grill flesh-side down for a further
1-2 minutes. Drizzle with olive oil and serve with
the lemon quarters.

Grilled flattened sardines (Recipe 22)

CHAPTER THREE
ROASTED & BAKED FISH

23 Whole sea bass baked in salt

1 x 2.5kg Sea bass, not scaled • 3.5kg Coarse preserving salt • 1 Lemon, sliced, plus 2 lemons, halved • 50g Fennel stalks

Preheat the oven to 200°C/Gas Mark 6.

Put the lemon slices and fennel stalks in the cavity of the fish. Cover the bottom of a baking dish with half the salt and lay the bass on it. Cover the fish completely with the remaining salt, in a layer about 1.5cm thick. Do not worry if the head and tail protrude. Sprinkle the surface of the salt with a little water.

Place the fish in the preheated oven. After 20 minutes, insert a skewer into the fish. If the tip of the skewer is warm, the fish is cooked.

Allow to cool for 5 minutes, then crack open the salt crust and remove it, ensuring that no salt remains on the flesh of the fish. Carefully lift the fish out and place on a platter. Remove the skin.

Serve at room temperature with the lemon halves and Salsa Verde (see Recipe 80), Aioli (see Recipe 87) or Basil Mayonnaise (see Recipe 85).

24 Sea bass baked in a bag with vermouth and fennel

4 x 220g Sea bass fillets • 150ml Extra-dry vermouth • 2 Fennel bulbs, tough outer layers and stalks removed (keep the leafy tops) • 200g Unsalted butter, softened • 2 Dried red chillies, crumbled • Juice and grated zest of 1 lemon, plus 1 lemon cut into quarters

Preheat the oven to 200°C/Gas Mark 6.

Cut the fennel bulbs lengthways into 1cm-thick slices. Cook in boiling salted water for 4 minutes, then drain and cool.

Make 4 rectangles of doubled foil, dull side out. Smear each generously with butter, then season with salt and pepper. Place a fillet in the middle of one half of each piece of foil and cover with a few slices of fennel. Scatter with the dried chillies, lemon zest and a few bits of fennel herb. Place a knob of butter on the fish. Fold the other half of the foil over the fish and fold to seal each side, leaving the top open. Pour a little vermouth and lemon juice into each, then seal the edges to make a loose, but airtight, package.

Put the bags on a baking tray and place in the preheated oven. Bake for 15 minutes or until the bags inflate. Split open each bag and serve.

Sea bass baked in a bag with vermouth and fennel (Recipe 24)

25 Roasted monkfish with anchovy and rosemary

2kg Monkfish tail • 8 Anchovy fillets • 2 Rosemary sprigs • 2 Lemons, 1 cut into quarters • Extra virgin olive oil

Preheat the oven to 220°C/Gas Mark 7.

Cut 1 of the lemons across into fine slices. Season and drizzle with olive oil. Heat an oven tray and drizzle it with olive oil. Place the rosemary sprigs on the tray and the fish on top. Cover with the lemon slices and then the anchovies. Season.

Place the fish in the preheated oven and cook for 20 minutes. To test for doneness, pierce with a sharp knife; the juices should be opaque. Serve with the lemon quarters.

26 Monkfish baked in a bag

4 x 220g Monkfish fillets • 2 tbs Rosemary leaves • 3 Garlic cloves, peeled and cut into slivers • 100g Unsalted butter, melted • 4 tbs Crème fraîche • 8 tbs Extra-dry white vermouth

Preheat the oven to 200°C/Gas Mark 6.

With a sharp knife, make tiny slits evenly all over the monkfish and insert 2-3 rosemary leaves, a sliver of garlic and some salt and pepper halfway into each.

Make 4 rectangles of doubled foil, dull side out. Brush with melted butter and place a piece of monkfish in the centre of one half of each piece. Put 1 tbs of crème fraîche on top. Fold the other half of the foil over the monkfish and fold to seal each side, leaving the top open. Pour 2 tbs of vermouth into each 'parcel' and seal well. It is essential for the packages to be airtight to stop the steam escaping.

Place the bags on a baking tray and bake at the top of the preheated oven for 20 minutes. Serve immediately, with the juices.

27 Roasted red mullet with white wine

8 x 200g Red mullet, scaled and cleaned • 250ml White wine • 2 tbs Finely chopped flat-leaf parsley • 3 Garlic cloves, peeled and finely chopped • Bruschetta, to serve (see Recipe 2) • I Lemon, cut into quarters • Extra virgin olive oil

Preheat the oven to 230°C/Gas Mark 8.

In a small frying pan, heat 6 tbs of olive oil, add the parsley and chopped garlic and fry over a low heat until soft.

Put the mullet in a roasting tin, then pour in the wine and the oil, parsley and garlic mixture. Place over a moderate heat and bring to the boil. Put in the preheated oven for 10 minutes.

Put one bruschetta and 2 red mullet on each plate and serve with the lemon quarters.

28 Red mullet baked in a bag with trevise

4 x 500g Red mullet, scaled and cleaned • 2 Small trevise or radicchio heads • 75g Butter • 2 Garlic cloves, peeled and cut into fine slivers • 200g Fresh porcini mushrooms, wiped clean with a damp cloth and sliced • 4 Sprigs of thyme • 2 Lemons, cut into quarters • Extra virgin olive oil

Preheat the oven to 230°C/Gas Mark 8.

Heat the butter in a pan and fry the garlic until light brown. Add the sliced porcini, season with salt and pepper and fry, shaking the pan, for 5 minutes.

Make 4 rectangles of doubled foil, dull side out, and brush with oil. Place 3 or 4 trevise leaves in the centre of one half of each piece of foil and add 2 slices of porcini, a little of the melted butter from the pan and some seasoning. Place the mullet on top with a sprig of thyme inside. Put some porcini slices on top with a few trevise leaves and a little more melted butter. Fold the other half of the foil over and seal the edges to make a loose, but airtight, package.

Place the packages on a baking tray and bake for 10-15 minutes. Remove the mullet from the foil and serve with the lemon quarters.

Red mullet baked in a bag with trevise (Recipe 28)

29 Roasted red mullet with olives, capers and tomatoes

4 x 500g Red mullet, scaled and cleaned • 50g Black olives, stoned • 50g Salted capers, rinsed of all their salt • 400g Ripe cherry tomatoes, halved and squeezed to remove juice and seeds • 2 Lemons, thinly sliced • 2 tbs Marjoram leaves • 3 Garlic cloves, peeled and finely chopped • 75ml White wine • Extra virgin olive oil

Preheat the oven to 150°C/Gas Mark 2.

Season the cavity and the outside of each fish and put 2 slices of lemon inside. Gently heat 60ml olive oil in a roasting pan large enough to contain the fish.

Place the fish carefully in the pan and cook over a low heat for 1 minute, just to sear the skin. Do not turn the fish over, as the skin is very thin and will tear. Roast in the preheated oven for 10 minutes.

Remove from the oven and return to the heat. Add the capers, olives, tomatoes, marjoram and garlic. Pour over a little oil and the white wine. Serve with the juices from the pan.

30 Roasted red mullet marinated with bay

4 x 500g Red mullet • 30 Fresh bay leaves • 4 Garlic cloves, peeled and finely sliced • 1 Lemon, cut into quarters • Extra virgin olive oil

Make 3 cuts in one side of each fish and push a bay leaf and a piece of garlic into each cut. Do the same on the other side. Place a few leaves inside each fish and season. Put in a dish and pour over a generous amount of olive oil. Cover and marinate for an hour or longer.

Preheat the oven to 220°C/Gas Mark 7.

Put the mullet on an ovenproof baking tray and cover with the remaining bay leaves. Place foil over loosely and bake for 20 minutes, removing the foil during the last few minutes. Serve with the lemon quarters.

31 Whole salmon baked in salt

Serves 8

1 x 4kg Whole wild salmon, scaled and cleaned • 5-6kg Natural coarse sea salt • 1 Large bunch of fresh fennel leaves and stalks • 2 Lemons, cut into quarters

Preheat the oven to 220°C/Gas Mark 7.

Season the salmon well on the inside only. Stuff the cavity with the fennel leaves and stalks. »

« Cover the bottom of a large roasting tray with a layer of salt 1 cm deep. Place the salmon on the salt. Cover the fish with the remainder of the salt so that it is completely covered by at least 1 cm all over. Do not worry if the head and tail protrude. Sprinkle the surface of the salt with a little water.

Place the salmon in the preheated oven. After 20 minutes, insert a skewer into the fish at a place where the flesh is thickest. If the tip of the skewer is warm, the salmon is cooked. Remove from the oven and allow to cool.

Break off the salt crust from the top of the fish. The skin should have stuck to the salt and come away as you do this. Gently lift the whole fish out of the roasting tray. Peel away any skin and salt stuck to the underside and place the fish on a board.

Serve at room temperature with the lemon quarters and Salsa Verde (see Recipe 80), Basil Mayonnaise (see Recipe 85) or Anchovy and Caper Mayonnaise (see Recipe 86).

---

32 Sea bass with porcini and thyme baked in a bag

4 x 220g Sea bass fillets • 20g Dried porcini mushrooms, soaked in 100ml hot water for 10 minutes • 8 Sprigs of thyme • 150g Unsalted butter • 2 Garlic cloves, peeled and finely sliced • Extra virgin olive oil

Preheat the oven to 200-230°C/Gas Mark 6-8.

For the porcini: drain the porcini, reserving the water. Rinse the porcini in a sieve under a running tap to remove any grit. Cut off any hard bits and chop roughly. Strain the soaking liquid through a sieve lined with kitchen paper.

Melt 50g of the butter in a thick-bottomed frying pan, add the garlic and fry until soft, then add the porcini. Cook gently, stirring, for 5 minutes to combine the flavours, then add 4 tbs of the porcini liquid. Simmer, stirring, until it has been absorbed, then add the remainder of the liquid. Simmer until the liquid has reduced to a thick sauce and the mushrooms are cooked. Season generously.

Make 4 rectangles of doubled foil, dull side out. Brush with oil and sprinkle with salt and pepper. Place a fillet in the middle of one half of each piece, skin-side down. Put a few porcini, a couple of thyme sprigs and a knob of butter on top. Moisten with a little of the porcini juices. Fold the other half of the foil over and seal the edges so that the parcel is loose but completely airtight.

Put the bags on a baking tray and bake in the preheated oven for 15 minutes. The foil will puff up. Remove from the oven, split open each bag, and place the fish on warm plates with the juices spooned over.

Sea bass with porcini and thyme baked in a bag (Recipe 32)

33   Whole turbot baked in salt

I x 2.5-3.5kg Whole turbot, head and tail intact, gills and roe removed • 3.5kg Natural coarse sea salt • I Bunch of rosemary • 2 Lemons, halved • Aged balsamic vinegar • Extra virgin olive oil

Preheat the oven to 220°C/Gas Mark 7.

Use a large baking tray that will hold the turbot snugly. Cover the bottom with half of the salt, in a layer at least I cm deep, and place the turbot on top. Push the rosemary into the cavity and completely cover the fish with the remainder of the salt, in a layer about 1.5cm thick. Do not worry if the head and tail protrude. Sprinkle the surface of the salt with a little water.

Place in the preheated oven. After 20 minutes, insert a skewer into the centre of the fish. If the tip of the skewer is warm, the turbot is cooked.

Allow to cool for 5 minutes, then crack open the salt crust. Carefully remove as much of the salt as possible. You will find the thick skin of the turbot will stick to the salt.

Divide the fish into 4 portions and place on plates. Drizzle each portion with balsamic vinegar and olive oil. Serve at room temperature, with the lemon halves.

34 Roasted turbot tranche

4 x 225-300g Turbot tranches • Juice of 3 lemons, plus 2 lemons, cut into quarters • 4 tbs Chopped green celery leaves • 4 tbs Chopped flat-leaf parsley • 8 tbs Salted capers, rinsed of all their salt • Extra virgin olive oil

Preheat the oven to 230°C/Gas Mark 8.

Brush the fish lightly with 2 tbs of olive oil and season. Place in one layer on a flat baking tray. Bake in the preheated oven for 15-20 minutes, according to the thickness of the tranches.

Remove from the oven and put the fish on serving plates. Add the lemon juice, celery leaves, half the parsley and the capers to the baking tray. Heat for about a minute over a high heat to combine the juices in the pan.

Pour the capers and juices over the turbot. Sprinkle the remainder of the parsley on top and serve with the lemon quarters.

35   Roasted Dover sole

*4 x 500g Dover sole, scaled and cleaned • 4 Lemons •
16 Dried bay leaves • 4 tbs Dried wild oregano •
Extra virgin olive oil*

Preheat the oven to 220°C/Gas Mark 7.

Cut 2 of the lemons into fine slices. Brush 2 flat baking
trays with olive oil. Scatter half the bay leaves, a few
lemon slices and some oregano over them. Place the
fish on top, season and scatter the remaining oregano,
bay leaves and lemon slices on top of the fish to cover
them. Drizzle with olive oil and bake in the oven for
10-15 minutes or until the flesh comes away easily
from the bone when tested with a knife.

Remove the sole from the baking trays and place
them on serving plates. Squeeze the juice from 1
lemon. Place 1 baking tray with its remaining herbs
and fish juices over a medium heat and tip in the
herbs and juices from the other tray. Stir in the lemon
juice, scraping up the bits from the base of the tin to
deglaze. Serve each sole with some of the sauce from
this tin, the bay leaves and the remaining lemon, cut
into quarters.

36   Roasted Dover sole with capers

*4 x 500g Dover sole, scaled and cleaned • 2 tbs Salted
capers, rinsed of all their salt • 2 tbs Marjoram leaves •
2 Lemons, cut into quarters • Extra virgin olive oil*

Preheat the oven to 220°C/Gas Mark 7.

Heat 2 flat baking trays, scatter them with salt and pepper and drizzle with olive oil. Place the fish on the trays, skin-side down. Scatter over the capers and marjoram, season and drizzle with olive oil.

Put in the oven and roast the fish for 10-15 minutes or until the flesh comes away easily from the bone when tested with a knife. Serve with the lemon quarters.

37 Roasted whole tuna loin

1.5kg Tuna loin in a piece, skinned and trimmed of sinew • 2 Garlic cloves, peeled and cut into slivers • 2 tbs Coriander seeds, lightly crushed • 2 tbs Salted capers, rinsed of all their salt • 2 tbs Roughly chopped mint • 250ml White wine • Extra virgin olive oil

Tomato sauce
750g Plum tomatoes, skinned, de-seeded and roughly chopped • 2 Garlic cloves, peeled and finely chopped • 2 Dried red chillies, crumbled • 1/2 Cinnamon stick • 1/2 tsp Dried oregano • 2 tbs Roughly chopped mint • 1 Fresh red chilli, cut in half lengthways, de-seeded and chopped • Extra virgin olive oil

To stud the loin, use a small, sharp kitchen knife to make horizontal slits along the entire surface of the tuna, about 5cm apart and 2cm deep. Into each slit push a sliver of garlic, coriander, salt and pepper, capers and mint.

Preheat the oven to 220°C/Gas Mark 7. »

« For the tomato sauce, heat 2 tbs of olive oil in a large, thick-bottomed pan. Add the garlic, dried chillies, cinnamon stick, oregano and the remaining coriander and fry until the garlic begins to soften. Add the mint, followed by the tomatoes and fresh chilli. Stir and cook over a high heat for 10-15 minutes. Season.

In a casserole or thick-bottomed roasting tin, heat 2 tbs of olive oil until very hot. Place the tuna in the pan and brown on all sides. Remove the loin from the pan and pour off excess oil. Pour the wine into the pan and boil to reduce a little, stirring and scraping.

Return the tuna loin to the pan and pour over the tomato sauce. Spoon some of the liquid over the top, half-cover the casserole and put in the preheated oven to bake for up to 20 minutes, or until cooked (rare).

Place on a carving board and cut into thick slices. Serve with the tomato sauce, sprinkled with the remaining chopped mint and capers.

38 Roasted sea bass with potatoes, white wine and thyme

1 x 2.5kg Sea bass, scaled and cleaned • 800g Waxy potatoes, peeled • 150ml Dry white wine • 3 tbs Thyme leaves • 80g Black olives, stoned • 60g Salted capers, rinsed of all their salt • Extra virgin olive oil

Preheat the oven to 200°C/Gas Mark 6.

Boil the potatoes in salted water until just cooked. Cut them lengthways into 1cm slices.

Line a baking tray with baking parchment, drizzle with olive oil and cover with the potatoes. Place the fish on top and scatter over the olives, capers and thyme, pushing some inside the fish. Season well.

Put in the oven and cook for 5 minutes. Pour over the wine and a little more oil, return to the oven and bake until the fish is cooked, about 20 minutes.

Fillet the bass and divide into 4 portions. Serve with the potatoes, olives and capers, and the cooking juices poured over.

39 Sea bass baked with potatoes and tomato

4 x 220g Sea bass fillets • 800g Waxy potatoes, peeled • 250g Cherry tomatoes, halved and squeezed to remove juice and seeds • 4 Rosemary sprigs • 8 Anchovy fillets • 450ml White wine • Extra virgin olive oil

Preheat the oven to 200°C/Gas Mark 6.

Cook the potatoes in boiling salted water until tender but still firm, then drain and cool. Cut the potatoes into slices 5mm thick.

Drizzle a baking tray with olive oil and cover with the potatoes and tomato halves. Place the rosemary on top and season. Place the bass fillets on top and put 2 anchovies on each fillet with some black pepper. Drizzle with olive oil.

Place in the preheated oven and bake for 6 minutes. Add the wine, return to the oven and bake for a further 6 minutes. Serve each portion with the juices spooned over from the pan.

40 Grilled then roasted whole sea bass

1 x 2.5kg Sea bass, scaled and cleaned • 2 tbs Fennel seeds • 2 Lemons, sliced • Parsley stalks • 2 Fennel bulbs, tough outer layer removed, sliced • Juice of 1 lemon • 75ml White wine • Extra virgin olive oil

Preheat the oven to 190°C/Gas Mark 5. Preheat a grill.

Put half the fennel seeds and some salt and pepper in the cavity of the fish. Brush the skin with a little olive oil and grill for about 5-6 minutes on each side, until it is lightly charred.

Place the lemon slices, parsley stalks, fennel slices and the remaining fennel seeds in a large ovenproof dish. Lay the fish on top and pour over the lemon juice, white wine and 5 tbs of olive oil. Bake for 30 minutes or until the flesh is firm to the touch.

Serve either hot or cold. This is delicious with Salsa Verde (Recipe 80)

41 Roasted langoustines

16 Langoustines • 2 tbs Dried oregano • 3-4 Dried red chillies, crumbled • Juice of 1 lemon, plus 1 lemon cut into quarters • Extra virgin olive oil

Preheat the oven to 220°C/Gas Mark 7.

Cut each langoustine in half lengthways. Sprinkle the flesh side with the oregano and chillies and season. Drizzle with olive oil and squeeze over the lemon juice.

Heat a large baking tray and place the langoustines on it, cut-side up, side by side. Roast in the preheated oven for 4-5 minutes.

Serve hot, with the lemon quarters.

42 Baked sardines

12 Large sardines, filleted • 100g Breadcrumbs • Grated zest of 2 lemons, plus 1 lemon cut into quarters • 200g Pine nuts • 3 Dried red chillies, crumbled • 4 tbs Finely chopped flat-leaf parsley • Extra virgin olive oil

Preheat the oven to 200°C/Gas Mark 6.

Brush a baking tray with olive oil and lay 3 of the fillets on it, skin-side down, next to each other. Sprinkle with some breadcrumbs, lemon zest, pine nuts, chillies and parsley. Season. Then lay another 3 fillets directly on top, skin-side up. Sprinkle with more breadcrumbs, lemon zest, chillies, parsley and pine nuts. Season. This is one portion. Repeat this process until you have 4 sandwiches.

Drizzle the sandwiches lightly with olive oil and bake for about 6-8 minutes. Serve with the lemon quarters.

43 Baked mussels with zucchini and yellow peppers

2kg Mussels, thoroughly cleaned • 3 Small zucchini, cut in half lengthways, then into 2mm slices • 3 Yellow peppers • 1 Red onion, peeled and finely sliced • 3 Garlic cloves, peeled and finely sliced • 2 Dried red chillies, crumbled • 150ml Dry white wine • 400g Tin of peeled plum tomatoes, drained of their juices •

3 tbs Salted capers, rinsed of salt, marinated in 2 tbs red wine vinegar • 6 tbs Chopped flat-leaf parsley • 1 Lemon, cut into quarters • Extra virgin olive oil

Preheat the oven to 230°C/Gas Mark 8. Discard any mussels that do not close when tapped.

In a thick-bottomed saucepan, heat 3 tbs of olive oil and gently fry the onion until soft. Add the garlic, cook until softened, then add the chillies, half the white wine and the tomatoes. Cook together for 30 minutes or until thick. Season.

In a separate pan of boiling salted water, blanch the zucchini for just 1 minute. Drain immediately.

Grill the peppers on all sides until the skin is black, then leave to cool in a plastic bag. When cool, remove the skin, seeds and any fibres from inside. Cut the flesh into 1cm cubes.

Use an ovenproof saucepan. Spoon the tomato sauce into the bottom of the pan. Add the capers, then cover with the mussels, zucchini and peppers. Pour over the remaining white wine, scatter over half the parsley and drizzle with olive oil.

Place in the hot oven and bake for 10 minutes or until all the mussels have opened. Discard any mussels that remain closed.

Serve with the remainder of the parsley, more olive oil and the lemon quarters.

Baked mussels with zucchini and yellow peppers (Recipe 43)

44 Roasted squid stuffed with chilli and parsley

4 Medium squid, cleaned • 5 Fresh red chillies, cut in half lengthways, de-seeded and chopped • 3 tbs Chopped flat-leaf parsley • 2 tbs lemon juice, plus I lemon cut into quarters • I Garlic clove, peeled and finely chopped • I tbs Dried oregano • 200g Rocket • Extra virgin olive oil

Preheat the oven to 230°C/Gas Mark 8.

Mix the lemon juice with 4 tbs of olive oil. Add half the chillies and the garlic and season. Stir in I tbs of parsley. Divide the mixture into 4 and stuff inside each squid. Mix the remainder of the chillies with 3 tbs of olive oil and season, to make a sauce.

Heat a large ovenproof dish and brush with olive oil. Sprinkle the oregano over each squid, season and place in the dish. Turn over, season and place in the oven. Roast for 5-6 minutes. The squid should be slightly brown. Serve with the chilli sauce, the remaining parsley, the rocket and the lemon quarters.

45 Roasted sardines

24 Sardines, cleaned • 500g Cherry tomatoes, pierced with a fork • Grated zest of 4 lemons • 50g Black olives, stoned • I Lemon, cut into quarters • Extra virgin olive oil

Preheat the oven to 200°C/Gas Mark 6.

Toss the tomatoes with 2 tbs of olive oil, season well and place in an ovenproof dish in a single layer. Bake for 15 minutes.

Choose an ovenproof dish large enough to hold the sardines in one layer and drizzle with olive oil.

Place the sardines side by side in the dish and season. Sprinkle over the lemon zest, olives and tomatoes and drizzle with olive oil. Bake for 10 minutes. Serve with the lemon quarters.

---

46 Roasted whole squid

*8 Medium squid, cleaned • 1 tbs Dried oregano •
3 Dried red chillies, crumbled • Juice of 1 lemon, plus
1 lemon cut into quarters • Extra virgin olive oil*

Preheat the oven to 220°C/Gas Mark 7.

Heat an oven tray and brush it with olive oil. When the oil is very hot, put in the squid and tentacles. Scatter the oregano and chillies over the squid and season generously. Finally squeeze over the lemon juice and drizzle with a little olive oil.

Put in the oven and roast for 5 minutes.

Spoon the juices over and serve with the lemon quarters.

Roasted whole squid (Recipe 46)

47   Roasted lobster with chilli

*4 x 450g Live lobsters • 2 Dried red chillies, crumbled •
1 tbs Dried oregano • Juice of 2 lemons, plus 1 lemon
cut into quarters • 3 Fresh red chillies, cut in half
lengthways, de-seeded and chopped • 4 tbs Chopped
flat-leaf parsley • Extra virgin olive oil*

Preheat the oven to 240°C/Gas Mark 9.

Place the lobsters face down on a board. Use a large,
sharp knife to split them down the centre. Remove
the little sac found near the head. Crack the claws.

Season the flesh of the lobsters with salt, pepper,
dried chilli and oregano. Squeeze over a little of the
lemon juice.

Place on baking trays and roast in the preheated oven
for 25 minutes. The shell of the lobster should turn
red and the flesh should be a light brown.

Mix 4 tbs of olive oil with the fresh chilli and parsley
and add 1 tbs of lemon juice. Stir to combine. Drizzle
this sauce over each lobster. Serve with the lemon
quarters.

48 Roasted scallops in their shells

*16 Queen scallops, cleaned but left in the shell •
2 Fresh red chillies, cut in half lengthways, de-seeded
and thinly sliced • 4 tbs Finely chopped flat-leaf
parsley • Juice of 1 lemon, plus 1 lemon cut into
quarters • Extra virgin olive oil*

Preheat the oven to 250°C/Gas Mark 10.

Heat a small amount of olive oil in a frying pan. Sear
the scallops in it, shell-side up. Turn them over, scatter
over the chillies and parsley and squeeze over the
juice of the lemon. Drizzle with olive oil and put in the
preheated oven for 3 minutes, or under a hot grill.
Serve with the lemon quarters.

CHAPTER FOUR
FRIED FISH

49 Fried scallops with borlotti

16 Scallops • Juice of 2 lemons, plus 1 lemon cut into quarters • 1 Fresh red chilli, sliced into 5mm pieces on the diagonal, seeds left in • 100g Rocket, chopped • Extra virgin olive oil

Borlotti beans
250g Dried borlotti beans, soaked overnight in a generous amount of water with 1 tsp bicarbonate of soda • 1 Fresh red chilli • 2 Garlic cloves, peeled

Drain the borlotti beans, rinse and put in a thick-bottomed saucepan with the whole chilli and garlic. Cover with cold water, bring to the boil and reduce to a simmer. Cook for approximately 45 minutes or until the beans are tender. Remove from the heat and allow to cool in the liquid. Season.

For the dressing, combine the juice of 1 lemon with 3 times its volume of olive oil and season.

Heat a thick-bottomed frying pan, large enough to hold the scallops in one layer, with a little oil to prevent the scallops sticking, then place over a high heat. When smoking, add the scallops, season and cook for 2 minutes on each side. Remove from the heat.

Reduce the heat. Add 1 tbs of olive oil to the pan, return to the heat and add the chilli. Squeeze over the juice of 1 lemon and shake the pan for a minute.

Toss the rocket with the dressing. Add the borlotti beans and divide between 4 plates. Place the scallops, chilli and any sauce from the pan on top. Serve with the lemon quarters.

---

50 Fried scallops with capers

16 Scallops • 3 tbs Salted capers, rinsed of salt • 2 tbs Sage leaves • Juice of 1 lemon, plus 1 lemon cut into quarters • Extra virgin olive oil

Brush a large, thick-bottomed frying pan with a little oil to prevent the scallops sticking, then place over a high heat.

When smoking, add the scallops, season and cook for 2 minutes on one side. Turn the scallops over and immediately add the capers and sage leaves, plus a little extra olive oil to fry the sage.

Cook for a further 2 minutes, shaking the pan constantly.

Squeeze in the lemon juice and serve with the lemon quarters.

Fried scallops with capers (Recipe 50)

51 | Fried squid with cannellini

1.5kg Squid, cleaned • 2 tbs Dried oregano • 3 Dried red chillies, crumbled • 2 Garlic cloves, peeled and finely chopped • Juice of 1 lemon, plus 1 lemon cut into quarters • 3 tbs Roughly chopped flat-leaf parsley • Extra virgin olive oil

Cannellini beans
250g Dried cannellini beans, soaked overnight in a generous amount of water with 1 tsp bicarbonate of soda • 1 Plum tomato • 2 Bunches of sage • 1 Garlic bulb, cut in half

Drain the cannellini beans, rinse and put in a thick-bottomed saucepan with the whole tomato, sage and garlic. Cover with cold water, bring to the boil and reduce to a simmer. Cook for approximately 45 minutes or until the beans are tender. Remove from the heat and let cool in the liquid. Season.

Heat 2 tbs of olive oil in a thick-bottomed pan until very hot. Add the squid. Immediately scatter over the oregano, dried chillies and garlic, and season. Turn each squid over and brown the other side – this will take a matter of seconds.

Add the lemon juice and half the chopped parsley, stir to combine. Remove from the heat.

Remove the beans with a slotted spoon and place them on a large platter. Scatter with the remaining chopped parsley and drizzle over some olive oil. Place the squid and their juices over the beans and serve with the lemon quarters.

52 Fried scallops with anchovies and dried chilli

16 Medium scallops • 8 Anchovy fillets • 1 Dried red chilli, crumbled • 2 tbs Flat-leaf parsley, chopped • Juice of 1 lemon, plus 1 lemon cut into quarters • Extra virgin olive oil

Brush a large, thick-bottomed frying pan with a little olive oil to prevent the scallops sticking, then place over a high heat.

When smoking add the scallops, season and cook for 2 minutes on one side. Turn the scallops over and immediately add the anchovies and chilli, plus a little extra olive oil. Cook for a further 2 minutes.

Finally add the parsley, then squeeze over the lemon juice and season. Place the scallops and anchovies on a plate with the juices from the pan spooned over.

Serve with the lemon quarters.

Fried scallops with anchovies and dried chilli (Recipe 52)

CHAPTER FIVE
FISH IN SOUP

53 Fish broth

Bones and trimmings from 1 turbot or halibut, including the head • 2 Red onions, peeled and cut into quarters • 2 Carrots, cut into quarters • 4 Celery stalks • 1 Fennel bulb, cut in half • 1 Head of garlic, peeled • 3 Flat-leaf parsley stalks • 2 Bay leaves • 1 tbs Fennel seeds • 6 Peppercorns • 2 Dried red chillies • 150ml White wine (optional)

Put the fish bones, head and trimmings into a large saucepan and add the vegetables, herbs and spices. Cover with 2 litres of cold water and add the wine, if using. Bring to the boil, skimming off the scum as it comes to the surface. Lower the heat and simmer gently for 15-20 minutes in order to achieve a fresh-tasting stock; do not be tempted to cook for longer than this. Season generously, then strain.

54 Fish soup

8 Live langoustines or prawns • 200g Mussels or clams, scrubbed • 2 x 450g Live lobsters, halved (see Recipe 47) • 350g Sea bream or red mullet, scaled • 1 Small red onion, peeled and finely chopped • 1 Garlic clove, peeled and chopped • 1 tbs Dried oregano • 2 Small dried red chillies, crumbled • 800g Ripe tomatoes, skinned, de-seeded and roughly chopped • 150ml White wine • 6 Medium waxy potatoes, scrubbed and cut into 5cm pieces • 4 tbs Chopped flat-leaf parsley • Extra virgin olive oil

Crostini
4 Slices of ciabatta bread • 1 Garlic clove, peeled •
Extra virgin olive oil

Discard any mussels or clams that do not close when tapped.

Heat 2 tbs of olive oil in a heavy saucepan large enough to hold all the fish. Add the onion and fry gently until soft, then add the garlic, oregano and chillies and cook for 2 minutes.

Add the tomatoes and continue to cook gently. When the tomatoes begin to break up, add the wine, bring to the boil, then add the potatoes. Cook for 5 minutes, then add the lobsters. Put the lid on and simmer gently for 4 minutes, then add the bream or mullet fillets and simmer for a further 5 minutes.

Add the mussels or clams and the langoustines or prawns. Season, replace the lid and simmer for 5 minutes. The shellfish should have opened (discard any that remain closed). Add the parsley.

For the crostini, grill the ciabatta bread on both sides. Lightly rub one side with garlic, season and drizzle with olive oil.

Serve the soup with the crostini.

55 Quick fish soup

300g Clams, thoroughly cleaned • 8 Langoustines • 350g Red mullet fillets • 350g Waxy potatoes, peeled and quartered • 2 Garlic cloves, peeled and sliced • 2 Dried red chillies, crumbled • 400g Tin of chopped tomatoes • 50g Fresh root ginger, grated • Juice of 1 lemon • 150ml White wine • 2 tbs Chopped flat-leaf parsley • Extra virgin olive oil

Discard any clams that do not close when tapped.

Heat 2 tbs of olive oil in a thick-bottomed pan. Add the potatoes, garlic and chillies and cook until coloured. Add the tomatoes and season. Cook for 15 minutes or until the potatoes are tender.

Stir in the ginger. Add all the fish, pour over the lemon juice and wine and season. Cover and simmer for 5 minutes. The clams should be open (discard any that remain closed) and the langoustines firm. Scatter over the parsley and drizzle with olive oil.

56 Spicy Sicilian stew

500g Mussels, scrubbed • 2 Garlic cloves, peeled and chopped • 1 tbs Coriander seeds, freshly ground • 1 tbs Fennel seeds, freshly ground • 400g Tin of chopped tomatoes • 250ml Dry white wine • 500g Red mullet fillets • 300g John Dory fillets • Crostini, to serve (see Recipe 54) • 2 tbs Chopped mint • 1 Lemon, cut into quarters • Extra virgin olive oil

Fish stock
250g Fish bones • 2 Bay leaves • 2 Garlic cloves, peeled • 2 Fresh red chillies • 150ml Dry white wine

Discard any mussels that do not close when tapped.

For the stock, put all the ingredients in a thick-bottomed pan, cover with 400ml water and season. Bring to the boil and skim. Simmer for 10 minutes, then strain and put aside.

In a thick-bottomed pan, heat 2 tbs of olive oil, add the chopped garlic and cook until soft. Add the ground seeds and the tomatoes and season. Cook for 10 minutes, breaking up the tomatoes. Remove from the heat and purée in a food processor.

Return to the pan and bring to the boil. Add the stock and the wine. Add the mussels, mullet and Dory. Season. Cover and cook until the mussels open and the fish is done, about 15 minutes. Discard any mussels that remain closed.

Place the crostini in 4 soup bowls and pour over the fish and the broth. Add the mint and a drizzle of olive oil and serve with the lemon quarters.

57   Clam and fennel soup

1.5kg Clams, thoroughly cleaned • 2 Fennel bulbs, tough outer layers and stalks removed (keep the leafy tops) • 4 Garlic cloves, 1 peeled and left whole, 3 peeled and finely chopped • 2 Dried red chillies, crumbled • 200ml White wine • 3 tbs Chopped flat-leaf parsley • 1 Ciabatta loaf • 1 Lemon, cut into quarters • Extra virgin olive oil

Boil the fennel in salted water until tender. Drain.

Heat 2 tbs of olive oil in a thick-bottomed pan, add the chopped garlic and chillies, and cook until soft. Add the clams, fennel and wine. Cover and cook until the clams open, a few minutes. Discard any that remain closed. Add the parsley and the fennel tops, and season.

Cut the ciabatta bread into 1.5cm slices. Toast, rub with the remaining garlic clove and put into warm bowls. Pour the clams, fennel and juices over and drizzle with olive oil.

Serve with the lemon quarters.

58 Mussel soup

2kg Mussels, scrubbed • ½ Ciabatta loaf, crust removed • Finely grated zest of 3 lemons • 2 tbs Oregano leaves • 2 Garlic cloves, peeled and chopped • 1 Dried red chilli, crumbled • 400g Tin of chopped tomatoes • 150ml White wine • 1 Lemon, cut into quarters • Extra virgin olive oil

Discard any mussels that do not close when tapped.

Pulse-chop the bread in a food processor to make coarse breadcrumbs. Combine the breadcrumbs, lemon zest and half the oregano. Add just enough olive oil to hold the mixture together.

Heat 2 tbs of olive oil in a thick-bottomed pan and fry the garlic and chilli until soft. Add the tomatoes and the remaining oregano and cook for 5 minutes, breaking up the tomatoes. Season.

Add the mussels, stir, and add the wine. Cover the pan and raise the heat. Cook, shaking the pan, until the mussels are open – about 5 minutes. Discard any that remain closed.

Divide the mussels between serving bowls. Scatter over the breadcrumbs, pour over the liquid and serve with the lemon quarters.

59 Porcini and clam soup

50g Dried porcini mushrooms, soaked in 200ml hot water for 10 minutes • 1.5kg Clams, thoroughly cleaned • 6 Garlic cloves, peeled and chopped • 1 tbs Dried oregano • 2 Small dried red chillies, crumbled • 400g Tin of peeled plum tomatoes • 250ml White wine • 3 tbs Chopped flat-leaf parsley • Bruschetta, to serve (see Recipe 2) • 1 Lemon, cut into quarters • Extra virgin olive oil

Discard any clams that do not close when tapped.

Drain the porcini and rinse in a sieve under a running tap to remove any grit. Cut off any hard bits and chop roughly.

Heat 2 tbs of olive oil in a thick-bottomed saucepan, fry the porcini for a few minutes, then add half the chopped garlic, the oregano and chillies and cook for a few minutes. Stir in the tomatoes with half their juices, breaking them up. Season and cook for 20 minutes to reduce to a thick sauce.

In a separate large saucepan with a lid, heat 4 tbs of olive oil, add the remaining chopped garlic and cook for a few minutes, then add the clams and the wine. Cover and cook for 5 minutes, shaking the pan to open the clams. Drain the liquid from the clams and pass through a fine sieve. Allow the clams to cool, then remove two-thirds of them from their shells. Add the clam liquid to the tomato sauce. Stir to combine and keep hot.

Add the clams, shelled and unshelled, to the soup. Season, bring to simmering point and remove from the heat. Stir in the parsley.

Place the bruschetta in 4 bowls. Ladle the soup over the bruschetta, drizzle with olive oil and serve with the lemon quarters.

60 Poached turbot

4 x 300g Turbot tranches • 3 Thyme sprigs • 4 Parsley stalks • 1 Celery stick • 3 Bay leaves • 1 tbs Fennel seeds • 1 Head of garlic • 4 tbs Black peppercorns • 350ml White wine

Tie together the thyme sprigs, parsley stalks, bay leaves and celery. Put all the ingredients except the fish in a saucepan wide enough to hold the turbot pieces in one layer. Add 1.5 litres of water and boil for 30 minutes.

Reduce to a simmer and add the fish. The fish should be covered by the liquid – top up with hot water if necessary. Poach for 10 minutes, then remove from the heat and drain.

Serve hot or at room temperature, with Salsa Verde (see Recipe 80).

Poached turbot (Recipe 60)

61 Chickpea and shrimp soup

400g Tin of chickpeas, drained and rinsed • 400g Peeled shrimps • 30g Dried porcini mushrooms, soaked in hot water for 15 minutes • 3 Garlic cloves, peeled and chopped • 2 tbs Dried oregano • 2 Dried red chillies, crumbled • 400g Tin of chopped tomatoes • Juice of 1 lemon • Crostini, to serve (see Recipe 54) • Extra virgin olive oil

Drain the porcini, reserving the water. Rinse in a sieve under a running tap to remove any grit. Cut off any hard bits and chop roughly. Strain the soaking liquid through a sieve lined with kitchen paper.

Heat 2 tbs of olive oil in a thick-bottomed pan and add half the garlic, the porcini, oregano and chillies. Season and cook for 4 minutes. Add the tomatoes and simmer for 20 minutes, adding a little of the porcini water to keep the soup liquid as the tomatoes reduce.

In a separate pan heat 1 tbs of olive oil and add the remaining garlic. When coloured, add the shrimps and chickpeas and stir though. Season and add the lemon juice. Mix the shrimps and chickpeas with the tomato.

Put the crostini in 4 bowls. Pour the soup over and drizzle with olive oil.

62 Whole crab with ginger

2 x 800g Live crabs • 70g Fresh root ginger, peeled and finely sliced • 8 Garlic cloves, peeled and finely sliced • 1 tbs Fennel seeds, crushed • 4 Fresh red chillies, sliced into diagonal rings • 4 Tomatoes, skinned, de-seeded and roughly chopped • 200ml White wine • Juice of 2 lemons, plus 1 lemon cut into quarters • 4 tbs Chopped fennel herb • Extra virgin olive oil

Cut each crab in half and then in half again.

Using a hammer, roughly break the shell on the claws and thicker legs.

Heat some olive oil in a large, thick-bottomed pan with a well-fitting lid. Add the crab, garlic, ginger, fennel seeds and chillies. Stir briefly and add the tomatoes, wine and half the lemon juice. Season generously, cover and cook for 10 minutes.

Add the fennel herb and the remaining lemon juice. Serve with the cooking juices in large bowls, with the lemon quarters.

CHAPTER SIX
CURED FISH

63 Grilled salt cod with lemon

4 x 250g Salt cod pieces, cut from the thick central part of the fish • 2 Lemons, halved • Extra virgin olive oil

Soak the cod in cold water for 48 hours, changing the water as many times as possible. The pieces will plump up as they soak and release salt.

Preheat a grill, griddle pan or barbecue.

Take the pieces of salt cod out of the water and pat and squeeze dry with a clean cloth. It is important that they are completely dry before they are grilled. Brush with olive oil and grill on either side until the cod is no longer transparent, about 6-8 minutes.

Serve with the lemon halves.

64 Salt cod with chickpeas, tomato and chard

400g Salt cod • 175g Chickpeas, dried and cooked, or 400g tin • 400g Tin of peeled plum tomatoes, drained of their juices • 400g Swiss chard, large stalks removed • 3 Garlic cloves, peeled and finely sliced • 2 Small dried red chillies, crumbled • 250ml White wine • 3 tbs Chopped flat-leaf parsley • Extra virgin olive oil

Soak the cod in cold water for 48 hours, changing the water as many times as possible. The pieces will plump up as they soak and release salt. Drain and cut into 5cm pieces.

Heat 2 tbs of olive oil in a thick-bottomed pan. Add half the sliced garlic, cook to soften a little, then add half the chillies and the tomatoes. Cook for 30 minutes. Season.

Heat 1 tbs of oil in a separate pan. Add the rest of the garlic and fry briefly. Place the cod on the garlic, brown on both sides, then add the wine. Reduce the heat and simmer for a few minutes, until the cod is cooked. Season with pepper and the remaining chillies.

Blanch the Swiss chard in a large pan of boiling water, then drain and chop roughly. Add the chickpeas to the tomato sauce. Heat gently for 2-3 minutes, then add the chard. Stir to combine then gently fold in the cod with the pan juices. Sprinkle with the parsley.

65   Salt cod with artichokes

*1kg Salt cod • 8 Small globe artichokes •
1 Medium red onion, peeled and chopped • 3
Garlic cloves, peeled and finely sliced • 2 tbs Finely
chopped flat-leaf parsley • 2 Dried red chillies,
crumbled • Juice of 2 lemons, plus 1 lemon cut
into quarters • 125ml White wine • Extra virgin
olive oil*

Soak the salt cod in fresh water for 48 hours,
changing the water as many times as possible. The
pieces will plump up as they soak and release salt.
Drain thoroughly.

To prepare the artichokes, pull off the tough
outer leaves until you reach the tender hearts.
Trim the tips and the stalks, then cut each
artichoke into eighths and remove any choke.

In a thick-bottomed saucepan, heat 2 tbs of olive
oil and fry the artichokes until they begin to
colour. Season. When the artichokes start to stick
to the bottom of the pan, add 150ml warm water
and scrape the juices from the bottom of the
pan. Cover with the lid askew and cook for 30
minutes, adding small amounts of water to keep
the artichokes moist.

Heat 2 tbs of olive oil in a large frying pan and
add the onion, half the garlic and half the parsley.
Cook until soft. Season. Add the artichokes, stir,
then cook, covered, for a few minutes.

Heat 3 tbs of olive oil in a large, thick-bottomed frying pan with a lid. Add the remaining garlic and fry. Place the cod in, skin-side down, with the chillies, the juice of 1 lemon, some pepper and the wine. Cover, reduce the heat and simmer for 5 minutes. Carefully flake the flesh from the skin. Add the cod to the artichokes and season. Drizzle over olive oil and lemon juice, then add the remaining parsley. Serve with the lemon quarters.

66 Bottarga with sea kale

75g Bottarga • 1kg Sea kale, trimmed of tough split ends • Juice of 2 lemons, plus 1 lemon cut into quarters • Extra virgin olive oil

Blanch the sea kale in boiling salted water until tender, about 3-5 minutes.

Drain carefully and place in a warmed bowl. Drizzle with olive oil and squeeze over the lemon juice. Season and toss gently.

Divide the sea kale between 4 warmed plates.

Shave the bottarga over each plate equally and serve, still warm, with the lemon quarters.

67 Salted anchovies with rosemary

*8 Salted anchovies • 1 tbs Finely chopped rosemary •
Juice of 1 lemon • 2 tsp Fennel seeds, crushed •
Bruschetta, to serve (see Recipe 2) • Extra virgin olive oil*

Rinse each anchovy under a slow-running tap to
remove any salt crusted to the skin, then carefully pull
each fillet off the bone. Discard the head and pull off
the fins and tail. Pat dry.

Put the anchovy fillets on a plate and sprinkle over the
lemon juice, fennel seeds and rosemary. Season with
black pepper and drizzle with olive oil.

Serve with bruschetta.

68 Salt cod salad

1kg Salt cod • 1 Small bunch of parsley, roughly chopped (keep the stalks for the stock) • 1 Garlic clove, peeled and squashed with a little salt • Juice of 3 lemons • 6 Fresh red chillies, cut in half lengthways, de-seeded and chopped • 200g Rocket • 225g Black olives, stoned • Bruschetta, to serve (see Recipe 2) • Extra virgin olive oil

Stock
4 Fresh bay leaves • 1 Fennel bulb, cut into 4, including the green parts, or a handful of fresh fennel leaves • 1 Head of garlic • 2 Carrots, peeled • 1 Small red onion, peeled • 1 Head of celery • 2 tbs Black peppercorns

Soak the salt cod in fresh water for 48 hours, changing the water as many times as possible. The pieces will plump up as they soak and release salt. Drain thoroughly.

Put the cod in a large pot with the stock ingredients and the parsley stalks. Cover with cold water, bring to the boil and simmer very gently until the cod is tender and flakes easily, about 15-20 minutes. Drain well and leave to cool.

Pull the cod apart into flakes. Put in a bowl and season with black pepper to taste, the salt-squashed garlic, a little of the lemon juice and 3 tbs of olive oil. Turn the cod over in the bowl to season each flake, then add the parsley and chillies. »

Salt cod salad (68)

« Put the rocket leaves in a bowl and toss with 3 tbs of olive oil and 1 tbs of lemon juice. Add the salt cod and scatter over the olives. Turn gently to combine. Serve with the bruschetta.

69 Salted anchovies with butter

8 Salted anchovies • 100g Unsalted butter • Juice of 1 lemon, plus 2 lemons cut into quarters • 2 Dried red chillies, crumbled • 4 Slices of sourdough bread • 1 Large rosemary sprig • Extra virgin olive oil

Rinse each anchovy under a slow-running tap to remove any salt crusted to the skin, then carefully pull each fillet off the bone. Discard the head and pull off the fins and tail. Pat dry.

Put the anchovy fillets on a flat plate and sprinkle over the lemon juice, black pepper and chillies. Drizzle with olive oil.

Grill the bread, rub with the rosemary, then butter generously. Lay the anchovies on top. Serve with the lemon quarters.

70 Smoked haddock carpaccio

*600g Smoked haddock • I tbs Fennel seeds, crushed •
Juice of I lemon, plus I lemon cut into quarters • Extra
virgin olive oil*

Using a long, flat-bladed knife, slice the haddock as
thinly as possible along the length of the fish.

Arrange the slices over each plate. Sprinkle with black
pepper and the fennel seeds. Drizzle the lemon juice
over and some olive oil. Serve with the lemon
quarters.

71 Smoked eel with celery, capers and chilli

500g Smoked eel on the bone • 2 Heads of celery, tough outer stalks removed • 50g Salted capers, rinsed of salt • 2 Dried red chillies, crumbled • Juice of 1 lemon, plus 1 lemon cut into quarters • Extra virgin olive oil

Cut the heart of the celery in half lengthways and shave finely, keeping a few of the tender pale leaves.

Mix the lemon juice with 3 times its volume of olive oil. Season and add the chillies. Put the capers in a small bowl and add 1 tbs of the dressing. Mix the celery with the celery leaves and the remaining dressing.

Skin and slice the eel and divide between 4 plates. Add the celery salad and scatter with the capers. Serve with the lemon quarters.

Smoked eel with samphire
and horseradish

500g Smoked eel on the bone • 400g Samphire •
100g Fresh horseradish, peeled and finely grated •
150ml Crème fraîche • Juice of 2 lemons, plus 1 lemon
cut into quarters • Extra virgin olive oil

Skin and slice the eel and divide between 4 plates.
Sprinkle with black pepper.

Mix the horseradish with $1/2$ tsp of sea salt and the
crème fraîche. Add the lemon juice.

Pick through the samphire, cutting off any tough
stalks. Wash thoroughly. Cook the samphire in boiling
water for 3 minutes or until tender. Drain and toss
with olive oil and 2-3 tbs of lemon juice.

Divide the samphire between the 4 plates, with a
spoonful of horseradish sauce. Serve with the lemon
quarters.

Smoked eel with samphire and horseradish (Recipe 72)

CHAPTER
SEVEN
FISH
IN SALAD

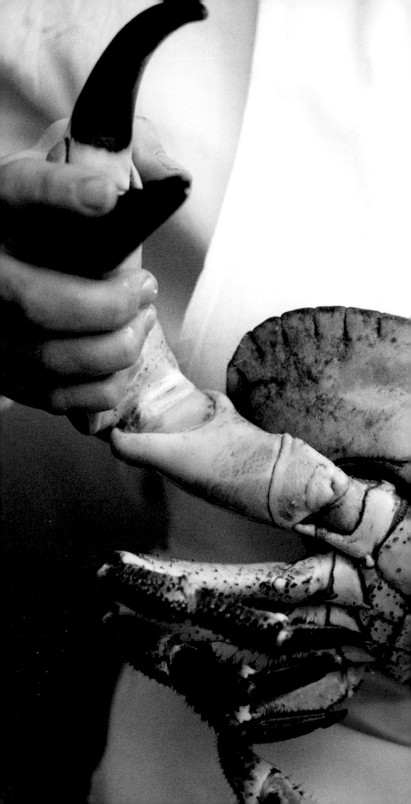

73 Crab salad

2 x 1-1.4kg Cooked crabs • Juice of 2 lemons, plus 2 lemons cut into quarters • 2 Medium fresh red chillies, cut in half lengthways, de-seeded and chopped • Bruschetta, to serve (see Recipe 2) • 1 Small bunch of green fennel herb, roughly chopped • 100g Rocket • Extra virgin olive oil

Break open each crab by pulling away the upper body shell. Scrape out the brown meat and put into a bowl.

Break the claws and legs from the body, crack and pick out the white meat, keeping the pieces as large as possible. Place in a separate bowl.

Mix two-thirds of the lemon juice with 3 tbs of olive oil and the chillies, then season. Add to the bowl of white meat. Season the brown meat with salt, pepper and the remaining lemon juice.

Generously cover half of each bruschetta with brown crab meat and half with white meat. Sprinkle over the fennel, then serve with the lemon quarters and rocket.

74 Crab with polenta

500g Crab meat • 2 Garlic cloves, peeled and chopped • 2 Dried red chillies, crumbled • 1 tbs Chopped flat-leaf parsley • Juice of 1 lemon, plus 1 lemon cut into quarters • Extra virgin olive oil

Polenta
350g Polenta flour • 1.75 litres water • Extra virgin olive oil

For the polenta, place the polenta flour in a jug. Bring the water to the boil in a thick-bottomed pan and add 1 tsp of salt. Lower the heat to a simmer and slowly add the polenta flour, stirring with a whisk until completely blended. Reduce the heat to as low as possible and cook the polenta, stirring with a wooden spoon, for about 45 minutes. Stir in 3 tbs of olive oil and season. The polenta is cooked when it falls away from the sides of the pan and has become dense and thick.

Heat 1 tbs of olive oil in a frying pan, add the garlic and cook until soft. Stir in the chillies and crab. Cook quickly to heat the crab through. Add the parsley. Season, then squeeze over the lemon juice.

Spoon the polenta onto warm plates and put the crab mixture on top. Drizzle with olive oil and serve with the lemon quarters.

75 Bottarga, potato salad

*100g Bottarga • 1kg Red Roseval potatoes, peeled •
1 Celery head, leaves intact • 2 tbs Red wine vinegar •
2 Fresh red chillies, finely sliced at an angle • Juice of
1 lemon • Extra virgin olive oil*

Bring a large saucepan of salted water to the boil, add
the potatoes and cook until al dente.

Drain the potatoes and cut into 1cm slices. Put in a
bowl and season. Sprinkle over the vinegar and drizzle
in 4 tbs of olive oil.

Chop the pale leaves from the inside celery stalks and
add to the potatoes. Discard the tough outer stalks
from the celery head. Cut the remaining stalks at an
angle into fine slices. Add to the potatoes and toss.

Divide the potato mixture between 4 serving plates
and dot the chilli slices over. Finely shave the bottarga
over each plate and squeeze the lemon juice over the
bottarga. Drizzle with a little more olive oil.

76   Bottarga and mâche salad

200g Bottarga • 300g Mâche leaves • Juice of
1 Lemon • 250g Cherry tomatoes, halved, or cut into
quarters if larger than 2cm in diameter • Extra virgin
olive oil

Mix the lemon juice with three times its volume of olive oil and season.

Put the tomatoes and mâche together in a large salad bowl, season and toss with the dressing. Immediately shave the bottarga over; use a potato peeler to get fine shavings. Drizzle individual portions with olive oil.

77 Langoustine with borlotti

16 Langoustines • 250g Cooked borlotti beans (see Recipe 49) • ½ Bottle of dry white wine • 6 Parsley stalks • 10 Black peppercorns • 4 Dried fennel sticks • 1 tbs Chopped flat-leaf parsley • 1 Fresh red chilli, cut in half lengthways, de-seeded and finely chopped • Juice of 1 lemon • 2 Garlic cloves, peeled and finely chopped • 150g Rocket, coarsely chopped • Extra virgin olive oil

For the langoustines, place the wine, parsley stalks, peppercorns and fennel sticks in a large, thick-bottomed saucepan, fill to the top with water, add salt and bring to the boil.

Add the langoustines in batches, bring back to the boil and cook for 1 minute only.

Remove the langoustines from the pan. They should feel firm – discard any soft ones. Cool.

Remove the shells from the langoustines. Toss the flesh with the parsley and chilli, most of the lemon juice (save 1 tbs) and some olive oil. Season.

Heat 2 tbs of olive oil in a thick-bottomed saucepan, add the garlic and cook until soft.

Drain the beans and stir them into the garlic. Toss the rocket with the remaining lemon juice and 3 tbs of olive oil. Stir into the beans and serve with the langoustines on top.

78 Poached langoustine with aioli

*16 Langoustines • 1 Fennel bulb, quartered • 1 Celery
head, halved • 1 Lemon, sliced • 1 tbs Black
peppercorns • 2 Bay leaves • 150ml White wine •
Aioli (see Recipe 87) • 1 Lemon, cut into quarters*

Bring a large pan of water to the boil. Add the
vegetables, lemon, seasonings and wine and return to
the boil. Add the langoustines, pushing them down so
they are submerged. Cover and cook until the
langoustines are firm, about 3-5 minutes, depending
on the size.

Drain and serve cold with salad, Aioli and the lemon
quarters.

CHAPTER EIGHT
SAUCES
FOR FISH

79 Anchovy and rosemary sauce

10 Anchovy fillets, finely chopped • 2 tbs Finely chopped rosemary • Juice of 1 lemon • Extra virgin olive oil

Put the anchovies in a bowl. Mix the lemon juice into the anchovies to 'melt' them, then stir in the rosemary and season with black pepper. Add 4 tbs of olive oil and mix well.

80 Salsa verde

2 tbs Finely chopped flat-leaf parsley • 1 tbs Finely chopped mint • 1 tbs Finely chopped basil (in summer) • 1 Garlic clove, peeled and chopped • 1 tbs Capers, rinsed of all their salt and chopped • 3 Anchovy fillets, chopped • 1 tbs Dijon mustard • 1 tbs Red wine vinegar • Extra virgin olive oil

Put the herbs into a bowl and cover with olive oil. Add the garlic, capers and anchovies and mix. Stir in the mustard and vinegar, season with black pepper and add more olive oil to loosen the sauce.

81   Olive, anchovy and basil sauce

*250g Black olives, stoned and roughly chopped •
6 Salted anchovies • 4 tbs Roughly chopped basil •
1 Garlic clove, peeled and finely chopped • Juice of 1
lemon • 3 tbs Balsamic or red wine vinegar • Extra
virgin olive oil*

Rinse each anchovy under a slow-running tap to
remove any salt crusted to the skin, then carefully pull
each fillet off the bone. Discard the head and pull off
the fins and tail. Pat dry and chop finely.

Combine the olives, anchovies and garlic. Stir in the
lemon juice, vinegar and 150ml olive oil and marinate
for at least half an hour. Add the basil just before
serving.

82   Green herb and pine nut sauce

*6 tbs Roughly chopped basil • 3 tbs Roughly chopped
flat-leaf parsley • 3 tbs Roughly chopped mint • 150g
Pine nuts, lightly toasted • 2 Slices of ciabatta bread,
bottom crust removed, chopped into breadcrumbs •
50g Salted capers, rinsed of all their salt • 2 tbs White
wine vinegar • Extra virgin olive oil*

Using a pestle and mortar, lightly pound the pine nuts,
then stir in the herbs. Add the breadcrumbs and
capers and mix with the vinegar and 5 tbs of olive oil.
Season well.

83   Hot anchovy sauce

*6 Salted anchovies • 2 tsp Finely chopped rosemary •
Juice of 1 lemon • 100g Unsalted butter*

Rinse each anchovy under a slow-running tap to
remove any salt crusted to the skin, then carefully pull
each fillet off the bone. Discard the head and pull off
the fins and tail. Pat dry.

Place the anchovies, rosemary and a pinch of pepper
in a mortar and pound to a smooth paste. Add the
lemon juice and stir well.

Gently melt the butter in a small saucepan and add
the anchovy paste. Stir constantly until warm but do
not allow it to boil.

84   Mayonnaise

2 Egg yolks • Juice of 1 lemon • Extra virgin olive oil

Gently whisk the yolks or blend at slow speed in an
electric mixer. Combine for a minute. Start adding
500ml olive oil, drop by drop, whisking constantly.
Continue until the emulsion is thick and sticky. At that
point, add a little lemon juice. Carry on adding oil and
lemon juice until you have finished both and have a
perfect thick mayonnaise. Season well.

85 Basil mayonnaise

6 tbs Basil leaves • Mayonnaise (see Recipe 84) •
2 Garlic cloves, squashed with a little sea salt

Crush the basil leaves in a pestle and mortar with the garlic and salt to form a wet purée. Add to the mayonnaise.

86 Anchovy and caper mayonnaise

5 Salted anchovies • 4 tbs Salted capers, rinsed of all their salt and roughly chopped • 2 Egg yolks • Juice of 2 lemons • 2 tbs Finely chopped flat-leaf parsley • 400ml Extra virgin olive oil

Rinse each anchovy under a slow-running tap to remove any salt crusted to the skin, then carefully pull each fillet off the bone. Discard the head and pull off the fins and tail. Pat dry and chop roughly.

Make the mayonnaise as described in Recipe 84, using the juice of one of the lemons only. Mix the juice of the second lemon with the anchovies and stir into the mayonnaise. Stir in the capers and parsley.

87   Aioli

¼ Ciabatta loaf, crust removed • 3 Garlic cloves, peeled • 1 Egg yolk • Juice of 1 lemon • Extra virgin olive oil

Wet the bread with water. Squeeze out most of the water. Using a pestle and mortar, pound the bread with the garlic and 1 tsp of salt to a smooth paste. Mix in the egg yolk and then 250ml of olive oil, drop by drop, until you have a thick sauce. Squeeze in the lemon juice and season with black pepper.

88   Almond aioli

100g Blanched almonds, roasted • Crusts from ½ ciabatta loaf, cut into large pieces • 4 Garlic cloves, peeled • 2 Egg yolks • Juice of 2 lemons • Extra virgin olive oil

Soak the crusts in cold water until soft. Squeeze dry.

Pound the garlic and almonds to a paste in a mortar with the pestle. Add the crusts and pound well to mix thoroughly. Mix in the egg yolks.

Pour in 250ml olive oil little by little, stirring with the pestle. When it becomes too thick to stir, thin with a little lemon juice. Continue to add the olive oil. Add more lemon juice to taste and then season. Aioli should have a rough, thick texture.

89 Grilled chilli sauce

4 Fresh red chillies • Juice of 1 lemon • Extra virgin olive oil

Grill the chillies until the skin is black and blistered.

Whilst still hot, seal in a small plastic bag or put in a bowl and cover with cling film. Allow to cool.

Pull the skin from the chillies, cut in half from top to bottom and remove the seeds. Put in a bowl, cover with 4 tbs of olive oil and season with sea salt and the lemon juice.

90 Fresh red chilli sauce

4 Fresh red chillies, cut in half lengthways, de-seeded and finely chopped • 25g Flat-leaf parsley, chopped • 1 Garlic clove, peeled and finely chopped • Extra virgin olive oil

Combine the chillies, parsley and garlic. Season with salt and pepper and add 120ml olive oil.

91 Salsa d'erba

6 tbs Finely chopped fresh herbs (mint, basil, marjoram, parsley) • 4 Salted anchovies • ¼ Stale ciabatta loaf • 1 tbs Red wine vinegar • 2 Garlic cloves, peeled and crushed • 2 tbs Salted capers, rinsed of all their salt and chopped • 1 Fresh red chilli, cut in half lengthways, de-seeded and chopped • Extra virgin olive oil

Rinse each anchovy under a slow-running tap to remove any salt crusted to the skin, then carefully pull each fillet off the bone. Discard the head and pull off the fins and tail. Pat dry and chop.

Soak the bread in the red wine vinegar and ½ cup of water for 10 minutes. Remove and squeeze out the liquid. Put the bread in a large bowl.

Add the crushed garlic, capers and anchovies and fold into the bread. Add the chilli and season. Add the herbs.

Slowly pour in 50ml olive oil until the sauce has a rough, thick texture.

92   Bagnet

4 Salted anchovies • ¼ Ciabatta loaf • 3 tbs Finely chopped flat-leaf parsley • I tbs Salted capers, rinsed of all their salt and finely chopped • I Garlic clove, peeled and crushed • Yolks of 2 hard-boiled eggs • I tbs White wine vinegar • Extra virgin olive oil

Rinse each anchovy under a slow-running tap to remove any salt crusted to the skin, then carefully pull each fillet off the bone. Discard the head and pull off the fins and tail. Pat dry and chop finely.

Soak the bread in water, then squeeze out the liquid. Using a fork, mix the bread with the anchovies, parsley, capers, garlic and hard-boiled egg yolks. Add the vinegar, 2 tbs of olive oil and some black pepper and stir to combine.

93   Oregano Salmoriglio

4 tbs Fresh oregano • Juice of I lemon • Extra virgin olive oil

Pound the oregano with I tsp of sea salt in a pestle and mortar until completely crushed. Add the lemon juice. Pour 8 tbs of olive oil slowly into the mixture. Add a little black pepper and stir to combine.

Variation
Thyme or lemon thyme can be substituted for the oregano.

94 Marjoram Salmoriglio

4 tbs Marjoram leaves • 2 tbs Lemon juice • Extra virgin olive oil

Pound the marjoram with 1 tsp of sea salt in a pestle and mortar until completely crushed. Add the lemon juice. Pour 8 tbs of olive oil slowly into the mixture. Add a little black pepper and stir to combine.

95 Salsa rossa

2 Red peppers • 1 Garlic clove, peeled and finely chopped • 1 Fresh red chilli, cut in half lengthways, de-seeded and finely chopped • 1 tbs Marjoram leaves • 4 Ripe tomatoes, skinned, or 250g tin of peeled plum tomatoes, drained of their juice • Extra virgin olive oil

Grill the peppers whole until black on all sides. Place in a plastic bag, seal and leave to cool. When cool, remove the blackened skin, then scrape out the seeds and fibres. Chop the flesh finely.

Heat 2 tbs of olive oil in a saucepan and gently fry the garlic until it starts to colour. Add the chilli, marjoram and tomatoes and cook for 30 minutes or until the sauce is reduced. Add the peppers and cook for a further 10 minutes. Season.

96   Etruscan salsa

¼ Stale sourdough loaf, crusts removed • I Garlic clove, peeled and finely sliced • I00ml Red wine vinegar • I tbs Each of finely chopped rosemary, sage, mint, thyme and marjoram • 75g Pine nuts • I Dried red chilli, crumbled • Extra virgin olive oil

Break up the bread, and put it in a bowl with the garlic, vinegar and 300ml water. Leave for 30 minutes. Chop the herbs together with the pine nuts. Squeeze out the excess water and vinegar from the bread and mix with the herbs. Pass through a mouli. Slowly add 150ml olive oil, and the chilli, and season to taste.

97   Black olive sauce

200g Black olives, stoned • I Fresh red chilli, cut in half lengthways, de-seeded and finely chopped • I Garlic clove, peeled and crushed • I tbs Fresh thyme • Extra virgin olive oil

Place the olives in a food processor and pulse to coarsely combine. Put into a bowl and stir in the chilli, garlic and thyme. Gently stir in 100ml olive oil and season generously.

98 Hot olive sauce

*300g Black olives, stoned • 5 Salted anchovies •
3 tbs Salted capers, rinsed of all their salt •
3 Garlic cloves, peeled and chopped •
150ml Double cream • Extra virgin olive oil*

Rinse each anchovy under a slow-running tap to remove any salt crusted to the skin, then carefully pull each fillet off the bone. Discard the head and pull off the fins and tail. Pat dry and chop.

Heat 250ml olive oil in a small saucepan until very hot. Add the olives, anchovies, capers and garlic. Stir and cook for 5 minutes, then remove from the heat. Add the cream immediately and stir until the sauce thickens.

99 Salsa rossa piccante

*3 Tomatoes, skinned and halved • 4 Fresh red chillies, cut in half lengthways, de-seeded and finely chopped •
1 tbs Dried oregano • 3 tbs Breadcrumbs • 1 tbs Red wine vinegar • Extra virgin olive oil*

Squeeze the seeds out of the tomatoes and chop to a pulp. Mix the tomato pulp with the chillies and stir in the oregano. Add the breadcrumbs and season. Mix in the vinegar and add enough olive oil to make a thick sauce.

100 Quick tomato sauce

2 x 400g Tins of peeled plum tomatoes • 3 Garlic cloves, peeled and sliced • 1 tbs Basil leaves • Extra virgin olive oil

Heat 2 tbs of olive oil in a thick-bottomed pan and fry the garlic until soft. Add the tomatoes and season. Cook over a high heat for 15 minutes, stirring to break up the tomatoes as they cook and prevent them sticking. Add the basil, drizzle with olive oil and season.

101 Tarragon sauce

100g Tarragon, stalks removed, leaves chopped • 4 Slices of ciabatta, crusts removed • 65ml Red wine vinegar • 5 Salted anchovies • 1 tbs Dijon mustard • 50g Salted capers, rinsed of their salt and chopped • Yolks of 2 hard-boiled eggs, mashed with a fork • Extra virgin olive oil

Tear the bread into small pieces and soak in the vinegar for 20 minutes. Squeeze dry and chop.

Rinse each anchovy under a slow-running tap to remove any salt crusted to the skin, then carefully pull each fillet off the bone. Discard the head and pull off the fins and tail. Pat dry and chop.

Very gently combine the bread, tarragon, mustard, anchovies and capers. Fold in the egg yolks, then gently stir in 120-175ml olive oil.

Index

The authors would like to thank Tanya Nathan, Ronnie Bonnetti, Fiona MacIntyre, Imogen Fortes, Sarah Lavelle, David Loftus and Mark Porter, and all the staff at the River Cafe.

1 3 5 7 9 10 8 6 4 2

Text © Rose Gray and Ruth Rogers 2006

First published in the United Kingdom in 2006 by Ebury Press, an imprint of Ebury Publishing, Random House UK Ltd., 20 Vauxhall Bridge Road, London SW1V 2SA

Random House Australia (Pty) Limited, 20 Alfred Street, Milsons Point, Sydney, New South Wales 2061, Australia

Random House New Zealand Limited, 18 Poland Road, Glenfield, Auckland 10, New Zealand

Random House (Pty) Limited, Isle of Houghton Corner of Boundary Road & Carse O'Gowrie Houghton, 2198, South Africa

Random House Publishers India Private Limited, 301 World Trade Tower, Hotel Intercontinental Grand Complex, Barakhamba Lane, New Delhi 110 001, India

Random House UK Limited Reg. No. 954009, www.randomhouse.co.uk

Papers used by Ebury Press are natural, recyclable products made from wood grown in sustainable forests.

A CIP catalogue record is available for this book from the British Library.

ISBN: 009191437X   ISBN: 9780091914370 (from Jan 2007)

Printed and bound in Italy by Graphicom SRL

Designed by Mark Porter Design, www.markporter.com

Copies are available at special rates for bulk orders. Contact the sales development team on 020 7840 8487 or visit www.booksforpromotions.co.uk for more information.